For Mum & Dad
Thank you for the upbringing steeped ... traditional music & dance

Endorsements

I'm really looking forward to Karen's well overdue book of tunes. As a fiddler, she combines great energy in her playing with an infectious rhythmic drive that makes it impossible to sit still and as a composer, she combines the best aspects of the older tradition with catchy new melodies that may end up being earworms (the good kind!). Making up tunes about where we live, what we see, and the people we know, helps make sure that the music has meaning for now and is part of a healthy, living tradition that renews while still maintaining a distinctively Scottish style.

Iain Fraser
Director at merlinmusicacademy.com

"Karen Steven's New Scottish Fiddle Tunes" is the Caithness fiddler's first collection of original compositions. Covering a range of tune types, including marches, reels, airs, and jigs, each of the 50 tunes demonstrates her mastery of the traditional idiom and command as a composer of new and inventive melody. The collection, featuring more than a few modern classics, would make a welcome addition to the bookshelf of any traditional musician or violinist.

Ronnie Gibson
Conductor & Leader of Aberdeen Strathspey & Reel Society

Published by Independent Publishing Network

2020

ISBN: 978-1-83853-482-0

Email: karen@karensteven.co.uk

22 Hollybank Place

ABERDEEN

AB11 6XS

Scotland, UK

www.karensteven.co.uk

Please direct all enquiries to the author

All cover photographs by Duncan McLachlan

www.studiograff-photo.co.uk admin@studiograff.co.uk

Photographs of Chloe Mackay, Eilidh Budge & Skye McLeod by Duncan McLachlan

Photograph of Ashley Swanson by Colin Campbell

www.colincampbellphotography.com ccphotography1993@gmail.com

Cover design, all artwork & typesetting by Kathryn Preston, Prestset Bureau

www.prestset.co.uk kathryn@prestset.co.uk

All rights reserved. No part of this book may be reproduced in any form or by any electronic or mechanical means, including storage and retrieval systems, without permission in writing from the publisher, except by reviewers, who may quote brief passages in a review.

Copyright © 2020 Karen Steven

Printed in Scotland

by

Bell & Bain Limited

Contents

Purchase of the book provides you with the below link to MP3 files of all 50 compositions.

https://soundcloud.com/user-10301333

Each tune is performed by Karen, once through, on fiddle, unaccompanied.

Introduction	7
Acknowledgements	8
Highland Council Commission 2000	9
Scotland's National Nature Reserves (NNRs)	15
Tanya Horne School of Highland Dancing Choreography	22
Tunes dedicated to Family & Friends	28
Style, Bowings & Ornamentation	51
Bonus Tune	53
Alphabetical Index of Tunes	55

Introduction

Although a tune book, it is as much about dance as it is about music to Karen. The two disciplines are very closely associated with one another. Karen first started out as a highland dancer, age 3 and went on to earn her teachers' qualification with the UK Alliance of Professional Teachers of Dancing Ltd in 1990. Betty Jessiman of the UKA described Karen as having "excellent musical knowledge". Raised in a musical household, Karen developed a repertoire of tunes, even before she started to learn violin in high school. In the days following highland dance competitions, Karen would hear the pipe tunes ringing in her ears. Fiddler Alasdair Fraser always says, "If you can sing it, you can play it". If the tune is in your head, you have already learned it. You simply need to transfer it to your instrument. Your memory will keep you in check if you make a mistake. The beauty of music playing in the Scottish tradition is that it is open to individual interpretation, therefore, the book is primarily free of bowings, ornamentations and variations, with the music providing the bare bones of the tune. Dictating bowings and ornamentations would be misleading to players, implying that is how the tune should be played, perhaps once, yes, but not every time. Players wishing to explore Karen's bowings, ornamentations and techniques are very welcome to contact her. She also recommends listening to the tunes from the book which can found on Karen's soundcloud see page 6 for details. Composing seemed a natural progression, and following some experimentation with composition in her teenage years, some of Karen's tunes featured in, The Nineties Collection. More recently, Karen was invited to submit some of her tunes to, The Aberdeen Collection, 2018. Dance, in particular, Highland and Cape Breton, is at the forefront of Karen's playing. She visualises dancers dancing to her tunes when she is playing, performing and composing, taking the same approach when playing for dancing, focussing on the dancers, to gauge the correct tempo. Much of the music in this book has dance at the heart of it.

Acknowledgements

To my rock and partner, the amazing Graham Mackay Sinclair, who's enthusiasm and positivity knows no bounds. I couldn't ask for a better, more understanding, interested and interesting person to share my life with. To Kathryn, at Prestset Bureau, can't thank her enough for her talent, creativity, passion for design and attention to detail. To Duncan McLachlan, Caithness photographer and musician, who took the photographs for my website and then, very kindly allowed me to use the photos in the book. To Tanya Horne, for loving dance and for choosing me to play fiddle and compose tunes for her dancers. To my sisters, Pauline and Maree, whose support, encouragement and enthusiasm for this project has been invaluable. To Alastair MacDonald, friend and fellow musician, for feedback and advice throughout and willingness and ability to 'top and tail' the tune recordings and enhance their quality. To everyone in the book, who has inspired me to write a tune for them. Special thanks to Donald McNeill (Loud-Trousered Multi-instrumentalist), there's nobody like him when it comes to donating time, expertise and assistance. To Eric & Helen Allan for their expertise and advice. To Iain Fraser, Ronnie Gibson, Chris Bell, Pete Saunders, Christine Martin, Bruce MacGregor, Stephen at Prestset Bureau and Joe at Webfactory. And, to you, I hope you enjoy some, if not all my tunes. Please feel free to contact me personally to discuss fiddle style, technique, bowings and ornamentations.

Thank you, Alasdair Fraser, the timing was perfect, 1987. For all the tuition, opportunities and friendship. There are numerous references throughout the book to Alasdair, Valley of The Moon and Sabhal Mòr Ostaig, which demonstrates the profound impact that meeting Alasdair has had on my music. Lucky me.

HIGHLAND COUNCIL COMMISSION 2000

The title of the commission, "Dances in the Wilds", comes from an essay written by Dunbeath author, Neil Gunn. The essay appeared in The Glasgow Herald on 31 May 1952.

Karen was selected to compose music, inspired by Caithness, to be performed at Eden Court Theatre, Inverness. Highland Dance choreography was incorporated into the medley from The Elise Lyall School of Dance, Wick. Karen was joined on stage for the performance by, James Ross on accordion, Wick and Niall Laybourne on cello, Halkirk.

The trio of musicians went on to record a CD entitled, "Dances in the Wilds".

Jig

The Wild Spell

The Wild Spell – Refers to a particularly bad storm in Caithness, September 1990, when many fishing boats were damaged or capsized.

© *Karen Steven*

The Brig o' Trams

Reel

The Brig O' Trams – Is a natural headland, coastal arch, situated to the south of Wick in Caithness. Starting out as 2 caves either side of the headland, weather and sea erosion has resulted in a single arched opening forming.

The Merry Men o' Mey

Jig

The Merry Men o' Mey – Looking out from St. John's Point on the north coast of Caithness, between Mey and John O'Groats, where many tides cross one another. The 'men' are the white horses produced by the crossing tides. This notoriously rough stretch of water is known as The Pentland Firth.

© Karen Steven

Reel

The Stroma Swelkie

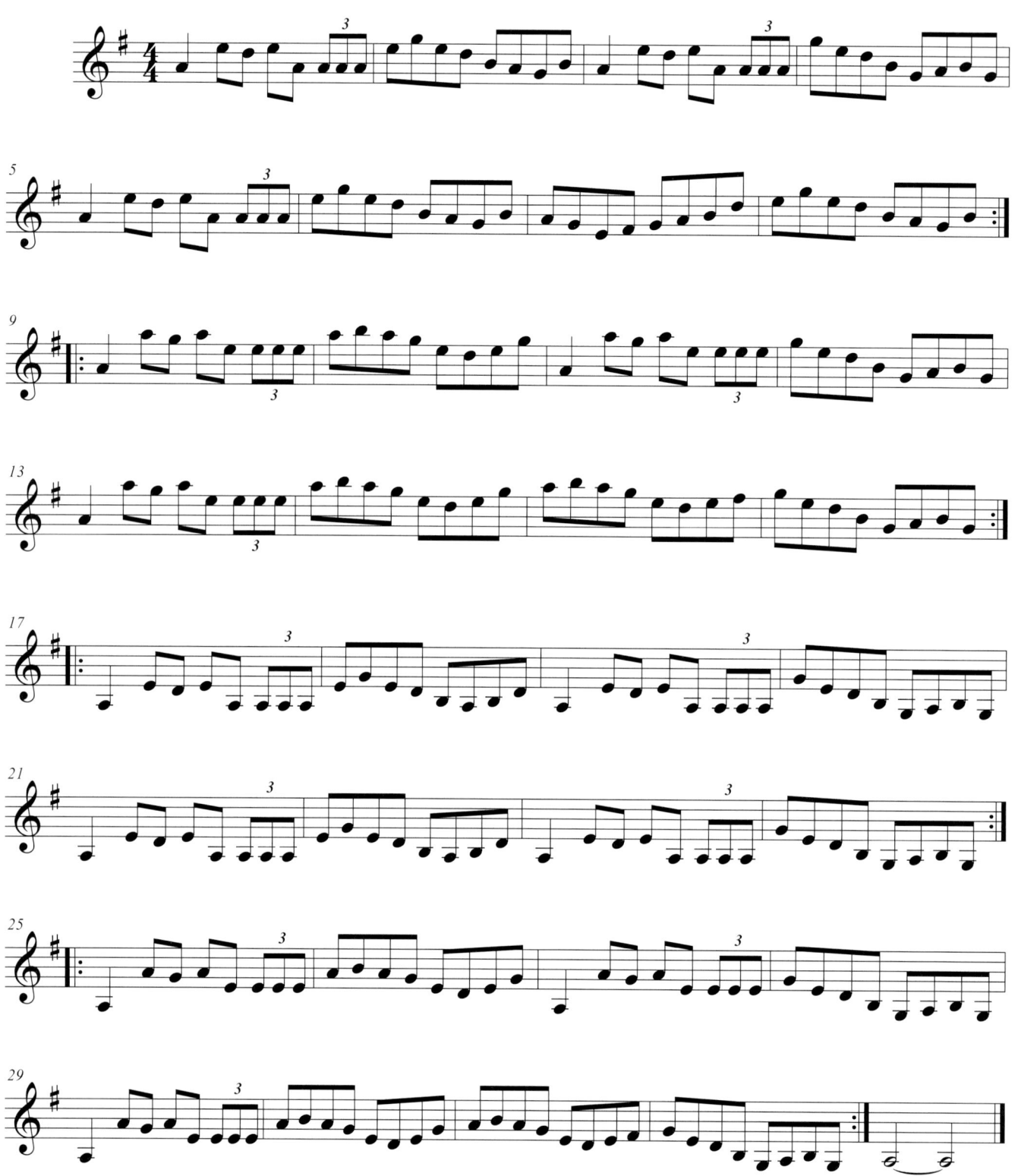

The Stroma Swelkie – Situated half-way between the North Coast of Scotland and The Orkney Islands, is he island of Stroma. The Swelkie is a busy whirlpool, where at the bottom of the sea, it is said, there are two millstones that grind the salt for the sea.

© Karen Steven

The Hills of Reay

March

The Hills of Reay – Are Cnoc Stanger, Keoltag and Beinn Ratha, their names evidence of both Norse and Gaelic presence in the country of Caithness at one time. At 795ft, Beinn Ratha is the tallest of the three.

© *Karen Steven*

Air

The Breck

The Breck – is a stretch of ground designated as common grazing, on the hill near John O'Groats, Caithness. It's an area of unspoiled beauty, comprising mosses, lichens, heather and peat. Looking east across The Breck, you can see the peak of one of the sea Stacks of Duncansby.

© *Karen Steven*

SCOTLAND'S NATIONAL NATURE RESERVES (NNRS)

CELEBRATING THE YEAR OF COASTS AND WATERS 2020

Tunes submitted to the Competition for Composers/Song Writers.

Promoted by Feis Rois, in conjunction with Scottish Natural Heritage (SNH).

At the time the book went to print the winning entries had not yet been announced.

© Karen Steven

Reel

The 4-Legged Volunteers

The 4-Legged Volunteers – Inspired by Caerlaverock NNR. Thanks to cattle on the reserve, suitable grass length is maintained, enabling waders, wildfowl and Svalbard Barnacle geese, and more, to breed and winter safely. The 2nd part of the tune is inspired by the meandering paths and boardwalks that guide visitors around the reserve, while being accessible for all levels of mobility. Do flock to Caerlaverock NNR but be mindful of protecting this habitat by following safety guidelines.

© Karen Steven

Tune for a Friend

Reel

© *Karen Steven*

Tune for a Friend – Inspired by Forvie NNR. Marram grass has an extremely important role in protecting coastlines. Its roots weave their magic underground, spreading and binding together, so that when weather targets the shores, the marram holds tight, helping to prevent coastal erosion. This 'friend' needs to be protected. The rise and fall of the notes in the tune reflect the effect that the wind has on the dunes at Forvie, just a few miles north of Aberdeen. The tune dips and dives, depicted by the slurred and tied bowings.

Reel

The Pillow is Popular with the Puffin

The Pillow is Popular with the Puffin – Inspired by Isle of May NNR. To gain access to the reserve, boats squeeze past the skerry, The Pillow, into Kirkhaven landing point. This, low sea stack provides puffins, seals and other wildlife with a sanctuary to relax and feed. The safe environment for wildlife is reflected in the smooth reel with controlled tempo. A versatile melody, simply play it faster and more rhythmically to depict the reserve on a wild winter's day.

© Karen Steven

Where Wildlife Flock to Rest and Refuel

Jig

Where Wildlife Flock to Rest and Refuel – Inspired by Loch Leven NNR. The aim for this tune was something bright and lively, to represent the arrival of birds from Northern countries who make the reserve their home in winter. Pink-footed geese, Whooper swans and breeds of duck enjoy this fresh water loch, less likely to freeze in winter than other Scottish lochs. The tune is packed with rhythmic expression indicative of the birds in flight as they migrate from Iceland, Greenland and Spitsbergen, Norway.

© *Karen Steven*

Reel

The Butterfly, The Beastie & The Bog

The Butterfly, The Beastie & The Bog – Inspired by Taynish NNR. Lots of notes in this 4-part tune to represent a reserve that is teeming with wildlife.

© *Karen Steven*

March for the Grey & Common Seal Haul-Out

March

March for the Grey & Common Seal Haul-Out – Inspired by Tentsmuir NNR. At low tide, the stunning golden sands of the reserve are revealed, a perfect spot for seals to bask.

© Karen Steven

THE TANYA HORNE SCHOOL OF HIGHLAND DANCING COMPOSITIONS FOR HIGHLAND CHOREOGRAPHY 2020

Tanya and Karen first started collaborating in 2017. While Tanya choreographs both group and solo new Highland Dances based on traditional steps, Karen arranges fiddle music to accompany the dancers, often composing tunes specifically for the individual dancers, for Tanya or for the dance school.

On 15th June 2019; Ashley, Chloe, Eilidh & Skye entertained at Skerray Village Hall Ceilidh. Raising funds for the hall refurbishment as well as Save the Children. The tunes on the following pages are a thank you to these lovely dancers of The Tanya Horne School of Highland Dancing Ltd.

In December 2019, Karen was joined by Chloe, Eilidh & Skye for a photo session to complement Karen's new website.

Thanks to Anne Taylor & Alastair Macdonald for accompanying Karen on keyboard, accordion & synthesiser & creating a recording for the dancers to practice and perform along to. Listen to the trio perform Dis-Dancing Highland Choreography Reel here https://soundcloud.com/user-553429985

© Karen Steven

Dis - Dancing Highland Choreography Reel
Reel

Dis-Dancing Highland Choreography Reel – A request from Tanya Horne School of Highland Dancing, Halkirk, Caithness to compose a tune for her highland dancing festival. 43 dancers choreographed a highland dance to this tune, which was presented on social media on 30th May 2020.

Tune for a Teacher
March

Tune for a Teacher – Composed for Tanya Horne, an inspirational dance teacher from Caithness. Tanya's dance classes focus on health, well-being, exercise, fun and hard work. She has danced for over 30 years.

© Karen Steven

Reel

Ashley Elizabeth Swanson of Halkirk

Ashley Elizabeth Swanson of Halkirk – With compliments to Ashley, who danced at Karen's fundraising ceilidh in Skerray on 15th June 2019. £1480 was raised for the hall funds and Save the Children charity on the night.

Ashley Elizabeth Swanson

© Karen Steven

Eilidh Ava Budge of Halkirk

March

Eilidh Ava Budge of Halkirk – Eilidh is a little firecracker. Smiling from start to finish, Eilidh performed for the camera brilliantly, at the December photo session for Karen's website. This tune is suited to the Scottish National Dance called Flora MacDonald.

© Karen Steven

March

Chloe Mackay of Halkirk

Chloe Mackay of Halkirk – Chloe took part in a photo session for Karen's website. She was a joy to work with, happy and professional. This tune is suited to the Scottish National Dance called The Blue Bonnets.

Eilidh Ava Budge

Chloe Mackay

© *Karen Steven*

Skye McLeod of Thurso

March

Skye McLeod of Thurso – Skye regularly posts videos on social media of her highland dancing. Every online post, Skye performs a different dance. Her improvement is remarkable and her enthusiasm for dance is inspiring.

Skye McLeod

© Karen Steven

FAMILY & FRIENDS ET AL

Where would we be without them.

The following tunes are dedicated to people who have been important to Karen over the years. These tunes are a small gesture of her appreciation for them.

© Karen Steven

Coffee Mate John

Jig

Coffee Mate John – Mr Bain was a lovely gentleman and friend to many. John donated numerous hours over the years to Feis Ghallaibh (Caithness Gaelic Music, Song & Dance Festival) helping to make classes accessible to youngsters. John was also partial to a coffee, hence the tune title.

© *Karen Steven*

Reel
Incitement for a Dormant Elkavox

Incitement for a Dormant Elkavox – The Elkavox was my dad's pride and joy, an electronic accordion he first heard Irish accordionist, Paddy Neary playing. This tune was to entice dad back into playing his box again. Due to health reasons dad is no longer able to play but he still enjoys listening to good music, his favourite tunes being, The Laird of Drumblair, The Spey in Spate, The High Level and The Jacqueline Waltz.

Reel
Je Bouge Mon Lit Pour Vous

Je Bouge Mon Lit Pour Vous – In 2012, musician, Yann Falquet (Genticorum) was due to visit Karen, en route to Orkney Folk Festival. When he missed his train connection in Inverness, Yann had to make alternative travel plans. Karen had moved a bed to the spare room for Yann.

© *Karen Steven*

Matty's Appeal
Strathspey

Matty's Appeal
Reel

Matty's Appeal – This tune was written and recorded to raise funds for the Taylor family, after Matty was involved in a motorcycle accident in Indonesia in 2011. Unfortunately, his travel insurance had expired and the family were faced with the enormous cost of bringing him home to The UK for treatment and rehabilitation.

© *Karen Steven*

March # McConnell's March

McConnell's March – For a number of years, Karen was itinerant fiddle player with the band, Dannsa. This tune was named after one of the 4 dancers in the group, Frank McConnell.

© Karen Steven

Millbank Road

March

Millbank Road – A very deserving tune for George Sinclair, one of the kindest and most helpful people you could ever meet.

© *Karen Steven*

March # Miss Elizabeth Christine Dickson's March

Miss Elizabeth Christine Dickson's March – Composed for Karen's mum who is a Scottish Country Dance enthusiast, as well as superb knitter and baker. A woman of many talents, Christine, as she is known, encouraged Karen and her siblings to pursue all things cultural, growing up.

© *Karen Steven*

Arrival of a Precious Wee Gem

Reel

Arrival of a Precious Wee Gem – Composed on the birth of Mara Gibb, Caithness, daughter of Stuart and Harriette.

The Pigini Playing V.P.

Reel

The Pigini Playing V.P. – Composed for Alastair Macdonald; engineer, accordionist, piano player, music producer, composer and Vice President of Decommissioning and Waste Management Oversight at AECL, Canada. A good friend of Karen's, who travelled to Cape Breton Island, Canada with her in 1986 as part of the group, The Caithness Junior Fiddlers, Alastair has assisted with this book project by editing all the audio tracks.

© Karen Steven

Reel

The Plant Scientist

The Plant Scientist – With Many Happy Returns, To Wendy, on her birthday, 2020, a dear friend and award winning, organic farmer.

© Karen Steven

The Sola Sisters
Reel

The Sola Sisters – Composed for the nieces of a great friend, musician and dancer, Sandra Robertson. Sola is a district of Stavanger, Norway, where the sisters, Synnøve and Emma live.

Trip to Lysefjord
Polka

Trip to Lysefjord – Written in appreciation of a beautiful landscape, north of Stavanger, Norway.

© *Karen Steven*

March

Valley of the Moon March

Valley of the Moon March – Composed for The Valley of the Moon, scholarship fundraising auction, Alasdair Fraser's summer school for Scottish fiddle, California where Karen has attended on 4 occasions.

© *Karen Steven*

Half Century Jig

Jig

Half Century Jig – Composed for Alison, herself a lovely, multi-instrumentalist, singer and dancer on the occasion of her significant birthday. Alison's passion and commitment to conservation, earned her the title of, Professor. She is a Senior Scientist and Baillie Gifford Entrepreneurial Research Fellow at The James Hutton Institute, Aberdeen.

The Winner

Reel

The Winner – Composed for Karen's partner, Graham, an inspirational figure in Karen's life. Graham is also very stimulating in his professional life, winning prizes for his work with young people, one being the Positive Ethos Award from Aberdeen City Council, 2016.

© Karen Steven

March

Inver Ceilidh

Inver Ceilidh – Composed for the Amber Fiddle Award, competition in 2011. Karen came 2nd, behind Shetland fiddle player, Gemma Donald who went on the win the competition 2 years running.

© *Karen Steven*

The Siblings
Reel

The Siblings – Where would we be without them – thank you, Pauline, Douglas and Maree, 3 very caring and sharing individuals.

Loud-Trousered Multi-Instrumentalist
Reel

Loud-Trousered Multi-Instrumentalist – Tune title lifted directly from his facebook page, Donald McNeill is a retired GP and donates enormous amounts of his time helping people. Karen owes Donald more than one tune for his generosity over the years. He is often seen at ceilidhs and gatherings, accompanying musicians but his music spans a variety of styles, with traditional Scottish being just one of them.

© *Karen Steven*

Reel

The Organic Veg Producer

The Organic Veg Producer – Composed for dear friend, Anne Taylor, who not only is a veg grower, but one of the most interesting, interested, talented musicians, kind-hearted and knowledgeable people Karen has ever met. And, Happy Birthday Anne, 2020.

© *Karen Steven*

Eilean nan Ròn

Reel

Eilean nan Ròn – Translates from The Gaelic as, Island of the Seals. Karen's granny Mina Mackay was born and raised on the island, before the family moved to the mainland, to Torrisdale, Skerray. She later married and set up home with Karen's grandpa, David Steven, in John O'Groats, where they ran the Caberfeidh Guesthouse for over 40 years.

West End Fiddler

Reel

West End Fiddler – Not only is Isabella a great fiddle player, she has many hobbies, which include; dance, ballet and golf to name a few. With an infectious personality, Isabella is the daughter of one of Karen's much valued friends.

© *Karen Steven*

Hornpipe

A.I. Willie Mackay

A.I. Willie Mackay – Works for Cattle Breeders in Caithness. For over twenty years, Willie has entertained as a compere at functions, gatherings, ceilidhs and concerts. Willie's enthusiasm and willingness to help and take part in events knows no bounds. He also is a great "Spoons" player.

© *Karen Steven*

Ashleigh's Jig
Jig

Ashleigh's Jig – Karen was guest artiste, along with guitarist, Peter MacCallum, Aberdeenshire, at the Ythan Fiddlers Rally in 2007. Proceeds from the evening's event were given to Ward 40 Neurosurgery, which holds a special place in Karen's heart. The winning bid on the night for this jig was Ashleigh.

Blas UL
Waltz

Blas UL – Blas translates from The Irish as 'Taste', with UL standing for University of Limerick, Ireland. Karen attended the Blas Summer School for Irish Music and Dance on 2 occasions and has dedicated this waltz to her great memories of being there.

© *Karen Steven*

Waltz

The Den

The Den – Is in the West End of Aberdeen, close to where Karen lives. It reminds her of Cragmont, Berkeley, California. North and South Rubislaw Den, 2 peaceful, residential parts of the city, with redwood trees lining the streets. The architecture and ambience there are a reminder of Karen's visits to San Francisco between 1988 and 2000, when musicians, Pate and Judy Thompson invited Karen to come and stay with them in their beautiful home in The Bay Area. Karen appreciated and enjoyed their hosting, friendship and music, during her late teens and early 20s.

© *Karen Steven*

Dannsa Hornpipe

Hornpipe

Dannsa – For a number of years, Karen was itinerant fiddler with the stepdance group, Dannsa, which translates from The Gaelic for 'Dance'. Karen toured Sweden with the group in 2004. In 2005, the group embarked on a tour of Scotland. Principal dancers, Caroline, Franks, Mats and Sandra choreographed a hornpipe to accompany the tune.

© *Karen Steven*

March

Mr & Mrs Allan of Drumossie

Mr & Mrs Allan of Drumossie – This tune is dedicated to Eric and his wife, Helen, who have offered fantastic advice for this project and their work as musicians and music publishers is admired by many.

© Karen Steven

Ebenezer Place

Reel

35 Years Strong

Reel

Ebenezer Place – Composed for The Lamonts' who run Mackays Hotel, Wick, one side of which is situated on Ebenezer Place, the shortest street in the world.

35 Years Strong – Composed for Wick Accordion & Fiddle Club's 35th Birthday. Karen was a regular at the club in her teenage years and grateful to receive a financial contribution for her trip to Alasdair Fraser's, Valley of the Moon fiddle school in California, 1988.

© Karen Steven

Reel

The Cracker

The Cracker – Another tune for Karen's dad, Donald John Steven (Eion). This was a Xmas gift to her dad, The Xmas Cracker, The Cracker, for short.

Reel

The Expert Carpenter

The Expert Carpenter – For Sean Bremner, teacher of Carpentry at North Highland College, Thurso. Much like learning a musical instrument, patience and attention to detail is required to be a good joiner.

© *Karen Steven*

STYLE, BOWINGS & ORNAMENTATION

As mentioned previously in the book, Karen has deliberately presented the tunes to allow players to interpret them how they wish. In this section of the book, however, players can read about some of the techniques that Karen uses to make the tunes sound more Scottish. In addition to reading about these ideas, players can go to Karen's soundcloud page.

https://soundcloud.com/user-10301333

The techniques shown on the following page are just some of the ones that Karen uses in her workshops. Others are better suited to live demonstration than via the book.

© Karen Steven

Style Tip – Bowing – Karen generally likes to play single-bowed style; the bow changing direction with every note, but beginning the bar on a down-bow. Occasional slurred bowings will be used, when needed, to enable starting the next bar on a down-bow. Karen likes to give attention to the up-bow strokes so that a similar amount of bow is used, thereby never running out of bow.

Karen's practice tip would be; using an open string, play a 4/4 timing, slowly to begin with. Focus on giving equal bow length to both the down-bows and the up-bows. Sometimes this means, anticipating the up-bow just a fraction early. Karen aims for the sound to be sympathetic to the Cape Breton style of fiddling and tries to avoid playing syncopated. If the sound is syncopated, you might be starting the up-bow too early.

Remember, to avoid running out of bow, a little speed will be required on the up-bow stroke, to bring you back to the correct place for taking the next down-bow stroke.

Style Tip – Strathspeys – On repeating a tune, Karen will sometimes introduce a 'jig' rhythm within the melody. As well as providing a contrast, this also creates the illusion of the tune increasing in tempo. It is also an effective technique when playing for step-dancing. Karen would advise fiddlers playing for step-dancing to watch the dancers' feet. This enables both the musician and the dancer either to mirror each other, or to complement each other in terms of rhythm.

Style Tip – Drones – When playing solo, especially unaccompanied, Karen likes to include open string drones. For example, If the melody note is an open D string, by pressing a little firmer with the bow, the open G string will also sound. There should be no need to consciously alter the angle of the bowing arm. Press a bit firmer on the strings with the bow, but increase the tempo slightly, to ensure that the sound remains pleasing. Also be aware that the drone note should not be the dominant note. Take care to ensure that the melody note is the stronger of the two.

Practice playing a scale using 2 strings. The scale notes will be more dominant than the accompanying drone.

Style Tip – Rhythm – New to playing in a Cape Breton style? Want to inject a bit of rhythm into your reel playing? Begin by taking a tune you are familiar with. Slow the tune right down and play it as a strathspey. Hear those snaps and dotted rhythms. Now, gradually increase the tempo of the tune, while still maintaining the feel of the strathspey. Try not to be too heavy with bow pressure. Ease up on some of the snaps and dotted rhythm, like a less is more approach. If you find yourself losing the Cape Breton, dance rhythm, just slow the tune back down to strathspey tempo again.

Style Tip – Triplets – Karen likes to substitute crotchet notes (1/4 notes) for triplets. For best effect, the advice would be to use this technique to vary the sound of a reel eg substituting a different crotchet each time. Being less predictable makes the music more interesting.

Style Tip – Tight Triplet – In order to maintain listener and dancer interest, Karen likes to vary strathspeys, by changing the occasional dotted quaver for a tight triplet. Basically, this requires replacing the single dotted quaver for 3 notes of the same pitch. Begin on a down-bow, close to the point of the bow. Slightly tense the bow arm when executing the technique. The timing of the triplet places emphasis on the 3rd note ie the 1st and 2nd notes of the triplet will be the shortest(quickest) notes, the 3rd note in the triplet will have more bow length and more time.

Style Tip – Chords within Melodies – are commonly played at the beginning and/or end of a tune. They can be effective at other places in your tunes. Using melodies from the book, build chords in where comfortable to do so. This will give your playing extra definition.

© Karen Steven

BONUS TUNE
TUNE 51

Karen composed the tune on the following page, one day after the book files had gone to the book printers. She was really pleased to find a way of halting progress on the order, so that this tune could be included. It is very fitting that this tune be dedicated to Duncan McLachlan. Duncan was booked to take the photographs for Karen's new website, but then very kindly allowed Karen to use some of them here, in the book.

© Karen Steven

Reel

The Christening

The Christening – For Duncan, to celebrate the opening of his new photography studio extension. Would be an honour to see this tune framed and hanging up there.

© Karen Steven

Index

35 Years Strong	49
A.I. Willie Mackay	44
Arrival of a Precious Wee Gem	35
Ashleigh's Jig	45
Ashley Elizabeth Swanson of Halkirk	24
Blas UL	45
Chloe Mackay of Halkirk	26
Coffee Mate John	29
Dannsa Hornpipe	47
Dis-Dancing Highland Choreography Reel	23
Ebenezer Place	49
Eilean nan Ròn	43
Eilidh Ava Budge of Halkirk	25
Half Century Jig	39
Incitement for a Dormant Elkavox	30
Inver Ceilidh	40
Je Bouge Mon Lit Pour Vous	30
Loud-Trousered Multi-Instrumentalist	41
March for the Grey and Common Seal Haul-Out	21
Matty's Appeal - Reel	31
Matty's Appeal - Strathspey	31
McConnell's March	32
Millbank Road	33
Miss Elizabeth Christine Dickson's March	34
Mr & Mrs Allan of Drumossie	48
Skye McLeod of Thurso	27
The 4-Legged Volunteers	16
The Breck	14
The Brig o' Trams	11
The Butterfly, The Beastie & The Bog	20
The Christening	54
The Cracker	50
The Den	46
The Expert Carpenter	50
The Hills of Reay	13
The Merry Men o' Mey	11
The Organic Veg Producer	42
The Pigini Playing V.P.	35
The Pillow is Popular with the Puffin	18
The Plant Scientist	36
The Siblings	41
The Sola Sisters	37
The Stroma Swelkie	12
The Wild Spell	10
The Winner	39
Trip to Lysefjord	37
Tune for a Friend	17/18
Tune for a Teacher	23
Valley of the Moon March	38
West End Fiddler	43
Where Wildlife Flock to Rest & Refuel	19

© Karen Steven

Notes

Notes